freddy
the fork

ISBN: Softcover   978-1-5035-7045-0

EBook   978-1-5035-7044-3

Print information available on the last page

Dedication

I dedicate this book in memory of "My Mother Lula Avery" who also enjoyed
writing and who continues to inspire me.

About The Author

Robin Avery is a nurse and author of "Patrick The Peanut" and "Freddy The Fork."

She spends her free time with family, traveling, and reading. She has one daughter and one granddaughter. She previously worked with premature and ill infants at LAC-USC Medical Center.

*Patrick The Peanut" was published in 2014 and takes you into an imaginary world where Patrick finds himself alone in another world without his family but manages to survive the whole ordeal.

"Freddy The Fork" was published in 2016 and takes the readers into Freddy's world of curiosity and dreams.

Robin currently lives in Indio, CA, and continues to work as a nurse.

Page Blank Intentionally

After the lights were turned off in the kitchen each night, Freddy would climb out of the drawer and wander about. He would climb on top of the refrigerator, jump down on the stove, and run in and out of the kitchen cabinets.

SUGA

Freddy hated being closed up in the drawer at night. So he would sleep on the kitchen counter at night and return to the drawer by daybreak.

SUGAR

The drawer was very boring to Freddy, and during the day, he could hear the family with whom he lived moving about and talking. And when the drawer was opened, he could take a quick peek!

There were really good days when he would be chosen for breakfast, lunch, dinner & even a snack! Freddy really loved these days because not only could he spend long periods of time out of the drawer, but he could see everyone and hear everything that happened in the family.

On the days when he wasn't chosen, he would get very bored and daydream.
Freddy would imagine himself going out of the front door! Running around the
yard and playing with the kid's toys.

One night, Freddy was in a deep sleep on the kitchen counter when Ashley, the youngest family member, came into the kitchen for a glass of water.

Freddy didn't hear anything until she turned on the lights! But it was too late for him to hide; Ashley had seen him! Freddy ran behind the toaster, terrified!

Ashley could not believe her eyes; she had never seen a fork that could move around like she did, like a human, and so very fast! She slowly walked over and peeked behind the toaster, and at that same time, Freddy was peeking from behind the toaster, and Wow! They both received such a scare!

However, the fright soon disappeared, and amazement took over. Ashley inspected Freddy from his head to his toes. She noticed how cute and tiny he was. She thought about how he could be her secret that she would not share with anyone, and her best friend!

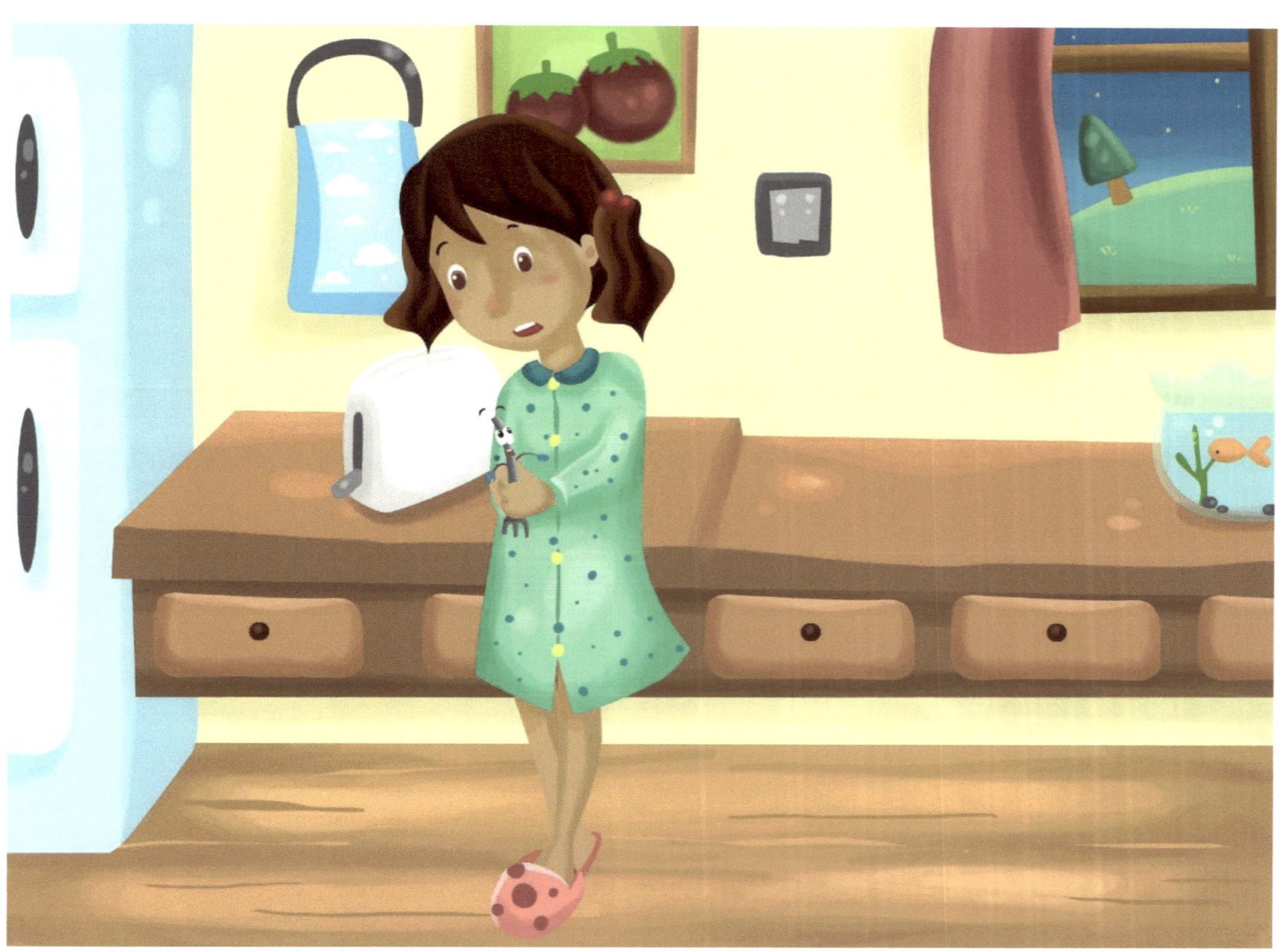

Ashley quickly picked Freddie up, and before he knew it, he was in her room, on top of her bed. Freddy loved the freedom he now had. He didn't need to sleep in that drawer anymore and Ashley treated him great!

Ashley loved having Freddy around because now she wasn't lonely when the older kids didn't play with her. She had a very own playmate and her very own secret!

THE END!